MODERN SEQUENCE

DANCING

A NEW APPROACH

T.A. WHITWORTH (CHESTERFIELD)

First published 1992

by

T. A. Whitworth, 42 Newbold Back Lane,
Chesterfield, Derbyshire, S40 4HQ.

ⓒ T. A. Whitworth

ISBN 0-9501927-2-4

Catalogue Number 793.33

Printed in Great Britain by:

B & S Print Specialists,
Storforth Lane Trading Estate,
Chesterfield, Derbyshire, S41 0QL.

AUTHOR'S FOREWORD

This book provides information on sequence dancing not readily available elsewhere. It sets out a strategy for learning and remembering modern sequence dances with some hints for beginners. A particular feature of the text is the development of a classification of dancing figures based on similarities between groups of steps rather than by individual dances as in most ballroom manuals. It is hoped that this will assist the dancer to recognise, remember and perform the various figures. The idea is not so much to teach people to dance as to supplement the work of the dancing teacher by providing material to study away from the dancing sessions. Practice and still more practice is the key to success. As Victor Sylvester says, "you should dance as you learn and learn as you dance". It is hoped that all sequence dancers will find something of value herein.

ACKNOWLEDGEMENTS

I am very grateful indeed to Mr. W. H. Share for advice and a critical reading of the manuscript.

My thanks are also offered to Mrs. S. Baker for the typesetting and Mr. J. N. Harrison for redrawing the line diagrams in the text.

To my wife Margaret with love.

A. M. D. G.

CONTENTS

CHAPTER 1

AN INTRODUCTION TO MODERN SEQUENCE DANCING

Sequence Dances

A modern sequence dance is a partner dance in which all couples on the floor perform the same steps at the same time. A dance such as the Melody Foxtrot or Mayfair Quickstep will have a set order of dancing figures arranged to fit a 16-bar sequence. The same type of music is used as for ballroom dancing but there is an introductory section of 4 bars to ensure that the dancers start off together.

Steps and figures from ballroom dancing make up the sequences but there is considerable interchange of figures between the various dances, e.g. the curved feather from the foxtrot is used in the waltz and the quickstep.

Types of Dance

Since the 1960's modern sequence dancing has settled into its present system with 15 <u>main</u> types of dance divided into 3 sections.

Modern Sequence

Old-Time		Modern		Latin-American	
OT Waltz	(1812)	Mod Waltz	(1922)	Rumba	(1948)
OT Tango	(1910)	Mod Tango	(1922)	Cha Cha Cha	(1954)
Saunter	(1914)	Slow Foxtrot	(1912)	Samba	(1930)
Blues	(1914)	Quickstep	(1925)	Jive	(1940)
Swing	(1914)				
Gavotte	(1840)	(Also Bossa Nova, Paso Doble, One-, Three-			
Two-Step	(1906)	and Four-Steps, Glide, Stroll, Rag, etc.)			

The dates give some idea of when the dances first appeared as ballroom dances in the U.K.

1

Sequence Dance Scripts

The steps for the 16-bar sequences are set out in dance scripts. These scripts are readily available for most sequence dances although there are no records for some of the older dances still performed in the clubs. (Dance scripts are referred to later on and a list of suppliers is provided.)

The number of scripts available for any particular dance depends upon its age and popularity.

Dance	Minimum No. of Scripts	Early Sequence Dances	
Tango	350	Square Tango	(1922)
Waltz (OT)	250	Veleta	(1900)
Waltz (Mod)	250	Waltz Catherine	(1956)
Saunter	200	Yearning Saunter	(1919)
Slow Foxtrot	150	Harry Lime Foxtrot	(1949)
Quickstep	150	Mayfair Quickstep	(1959)
Two-Step	100	Military Two Step	(1906)
Rumba	80	Rumba Royale	(1963)
Blues	80	Lingering Blues	(1929)
Cha Cha Cha	70	Jacqueline Cha Cha Cha	(1962)
Swing	70	Midnight Swing	(1962)
Gavotte	50	Butterfly Gavotte	(1950)
Jive	40	Jim Jam Jive	(1962)
Samba	30	Samba Miranda	(1961)
TOTAL	**1870**		

Old-time waltzes use different dancing figures and are played at 44-64 bars per minute; modern waltzes are played at 28-34 bars per minute.

The differences in style between modern and old-time tangos are more subtle: these dances are classed together in this table.

2

New Sequence Dances

Many sequence dances of various types have been devised over the years by dancing teachers and competition dancers both in the U.K. and overseas. Since 1975 a certain number of dances have been approved by the British Council of Ballroom Dancing (previously called the Official Board of Ballroom Dancing). Some 15 bodies are allowed to offer awards in Old-Time, Modern and Latin-American sections making some 45 new official dances in the full year. Dancers compete at the various festivals and the scripts of the winning dances are sent to subscribers as soon as possible. Within a week of the dances appearing many sequence dancers are able to perform them with reasonable ability.

Despite attempts to spread the competitions evenly throughout the year there is a rush of dances at bank holidays and a gap of 2 months around Christmas. It is notable that certain competitors seem able to catch the judge's eye. It is not at all unusual for a pair to win 3 or more competitions in a year. Of the 45 dances appearing in 1990, 13 were produced by 4 couples.

New Official Dances 1981 – 1991

Dance	No. of Dances	Dance	No. of Dances
Tango (Mod & OT)	74	Swing	20
Waltz (Mod)	60	Blues	14
Rumba	55	Gavotte	13
Saunter	48	Samba	10
Cha Cha Cha	45	Waltz (OT)	10
Quickstep	37	Two-Step	5
Jive	35	Others	2
Foxtrot	34	**TOTAL**	**462**

3

The Popularity of Sequence Dancing

In places where modern sequence dancing has caught on it must be the most popular form of ballroom dancing yet devised. Within easy travelling distance of a medium-sized town (population, say, 100,000) in one of these areas there may be 3 or 4 sequence dancing sessions each evening with occasional dances in the morning and afternoon. There are hundreds of regular dancers and an average attendance of 50 or more at a session is not unusual. Some dancers have been turning out several evenings per week for 20 years or more. Dancers can choose between an evening out with friends performing a few of the older sequence dances to a commitment of 7 nights per week mastering the new dances as they appear and working to improve their technique.

Some reasons for this enthusiasm are:-

(a) the wide range of dances available - more than 20 types of dance, at least 1,500 sequence dances.

(b) many more different dancing figures can be used since leading by the man is less important than in ballroom dancing. Figures moving against the line of dance can be brought in since everyone is moving the same way.

(c) sequence dancing is easier to learn than dance forms with free expression since the steps are repeated many times. Dancing can be learned by observation and lessons are not essential.

(d) the new dances produced every year give life and interest to the movement. Sessions are crowded as soon as they appear.

Other important factors are:-

(a) the availability of cheap devices for playing recorded music. Any group can now come together for sequence dancing given a floor and a leader. Dancers can attend several dances per week without costs being prohibitive. These clubs have been a stabilising influence and have provided opportunities for newcomers to learn the art. Club dances have been invaluable in preserving the older dances and promoting the best of the new.

(b) the general improvement in the standard of living. Older people are in better health, have more time available and often have a car to get to outlying dances.

(c) the high standards of performance set and maintained by the various professional ballroom associations. These bodies provide qualifications for teachers and students, monitor new sequence dances and give a firm structure to the movement.

(d) the efforts of the hundreds of dedicated group leaders and teachers who turn up regularly (often without financial gain) to play the music and lead off the dances. Often they have to prepare the room and tidy up afterwards. They are truly the backbone of the sequence dancing of today.

CHAPTER 2

LEARNING SEQUENCE DANCING

The choice of learning method will depend on what facilities are available and the ultimate objective - is the dancing to be mainly a social activity or will the aim be to master the new dances as they appear and acquire a good style?

Social (club) dancers often attend groups or tea dances where the simpler sequence dances are performed. They master the dances by careful observation and following people as they dance round. Many club dancers follow this method and get by reasonably well without formal teaching, dance scripts or much else; these dancers often have a great talent for performing and remembering sequence dances. The number of dances that can be learnt is somewhat restricted, however, and faults in style and performance may be picked up from other dancers.

By far the most common method is to join an elementary sequence dance teaching group. Some of the easier and more popular dances are "stepped through" and then practised by the class as a whole. The repertoire of dances is gradually extended with on-going instruction in technique and dancing style. Intermediate or improvers' classes include some of the simpler new dances whereas advanced classes teach the new dances as they appear.

There is not always a sharp distinction between teaching sessions and dances - all sequence dance sessions have some type of learning element. Most leaders will "step through" or call out the order of dancing figures for a new dance or an older one that has been partially forgotten unless the dance is a very formal occasion.

A Time Scale for Learning

There are so many modern sequence dances that it is unrealistic to expect to master them all. A more reasonable aim would be to be able to attend any local session, holiday dance or sequence dancing festival without feeling too much out of place. To perform most of the dances with reasonable style and to follow the rest without being a nuisance to others — this is a standard attained by many but not without a good deal of effort and some anguish at times.

Some dancers will be hindered by lack of time, shortage of partners, physical disabilities, illness or lack of facilities in a particular area. It will also take longer if the basic skills of ballroom dancing have to be acquired. To be used to dancing with a partner and be able to transfer weight smoothly from one foot to the other is a great help to the aspiring sequence dancer. All things considered, an average time of about 3 years seems about right, with continuing improvements in repertoire of dances and style as the years pass by.

First Year (Elementary)

Progress is rather slow for the first few months while the first dances are being mastered. It may be a very frustrating period for a slow learner to see others getting on well — persistence is required here. It is sometimes said that slow learners make the best dancers at the end. When a repertoire of about 10 dances has been achieved it will be possible to get in more practice at other sessions and things will move along faster. A good selection of the older dances is very useful since they come up regularly on all sorts of occasions.

Second Year (Intermediate)

More of the same with the introduction of some of the newer dances.

7

Third Year

If the first stages have gone well this is the time to try to master the new dances as they appear (some 45 per year). This process is simpler than might be thought, if several evenings per week are available, since the new dances are stepped through and played a great deal at the advanced sessions. Practice is certainly the secret of success - even the more accomplished dancers work harder as the new dances appear.

Private Lessons

Some teachers give instruction in sequence dancing in the period before the group dancing session. More rapid progress can be made and there are good opportunities to discuss difficulties and details of dancing technique. It is, however, more expensive and some slow learners may feel uncomfortable under the eagle eye of the instructor.

Another alternative is to take lessons in ballroom dancing. If the various figures are learnt correctly it is not too difficult to adapt to modern sequence. Although there is much common ground between ballroom and sequence there are distinct differences - the two styles cannot even share the same floor for a quickstep! Ballroom dancers aim to execute a limited number of figures in a dance such as a waltz or quickstep with a classic style according to the principles laid down by the various dancing associations. They usually work towards examinations and many dancing manuals are written with this in mind. Ballroom dancers design their own sequences of dancing figures rather than following a set 16-bar sequence. All sequence dancers must sooner or later give some attention to style of performance once they have passed the elementary stages - teaching by a qualified ballroom dancing teacher is, perhaps, the only effective way to attain a really high standard.

Repertoire of Dances

The number of dances in any couple's repertoire will vary from night to night with mood and circumstances. Average dancers might expect to learn some 50 dances per year making 150 at the end of the 3-year learning period.

The following figures refer to a recent modern sequence dancing festival.

Age of dance	Number of dances	%
Current year	55	47.0
1-year old	15	12.8
2-year old	9	7.7
3 - 10-year old	13	11.1
More than 10-year	25	21.4

The learning programme suggested here would cover nearly half the dances (current year) with possibly another quarter being accounted for by older dances learned in the first 2 years; the remainder could be attempted or sat out. Notice that the 13 dances played in the 3 - 10 years category were chosen from 327 new dances appearing in the period (only 1 in 25).

Sequence Dancing Sessions

Where modern sequence dancing is well-established there may be as many as 3 or 4 sessions to choose from each evening within a reasonable catchment area. It is important for the aspiring sequence dancer to choose the right level - too low a standard leads to boredom and lack of progress, too advanced a programme will lead to waste of time by missing dances and discouragement. As dancers improve they need to raise their standard and there is the problem of breaking ties and leaving friends behind. Eventually a more settled programme will be established but the sequence dancing situation is fluid and places rise and fall in popularity.

Types of Sequence Dancing Session

Type	Standard of dances	Music	Notes
Tea dance	E	Recorded or live	Elementary sequence dances with some ballroom dancing. Good for the beginner.
Dancing clubs and groups	I	Recorded	Dances led off by the organisers or other nominated couples. Entrance fee and a small annual membership subscription. May be outings, dinners, etc. Tea and biscuits often provided.
Licensed clubs	E I	Live (Organist)	No leader. Often free if you sign as a visitor. Small annual subscription if you join. Bingo and raffle also.
Teaching and semi-teaching	E I A	Recorded	Teachers usually lead off although others may be nominated. These sessions give practice in the dances taught.
Formal dances	I A	Live	May have a leader as well. Sometimes attended by dancing teachers with groups of students.
Dancing holidays	I	Recorded or live	Sightseeing in the day. Dancing sessions in the evening.
Sequence dancing festivals	I A	Live	Teaching sessions in the morning and afternoon. Formal sessions in the evening.

E - Elementary, I - Intermediate, A - Advanced

Remembering Sequence Dances

Remembering sequence dances is a big problem - it keeps the sequence dancers on their toes! Quite a bit of remembering is by reflex action - the legs go where they should without much thought. Practice is the key to developing this facility, and the ability to remember old dances and perform the newer ones should improve with time. This form of remembering can be helped (and sometimes hindered!) by using the mind.

Different dancers picture the sequences in different ways but there are one or two general methods of helping recall. It may be enough to remember one particular step or series of steps to jog the memory:-

- the aerial turn in the Eugene Tango;
- the pendulum points in the Quatro Quickstep;
- the hinge in the Charminster Waltz and Waltz Clinique.

Once a repertoire of dances has been established one of the best ways of remembering is by association - comparing the movements of one dance with another. This may be in very general terms:-

- Tiara Tango is the Square Tango backwards;
- Red Rose Saunter is the Together Saunter with lock steps.

Vague ideas of this kind often stick in the mind and many club dancers use this method of recall.

The basis of a better method of comparing dances is by noting similarities in the sequence patterns. Dancing teachers will often point out that the middle sections of the Emmerdale and Woodside Waltzes are very similar. A more precise way of putting this is to say they use the same series of <u>dancing figures</u>:-

Whisk, Wing, Open Telemark, Hover, Contra Check.

Of the 48 steps in the 2 dances, 14 are virtually the same.

Since there are only a limited number of dancing figures and new dances keep appearing, there must be some repetition of popular sequences.

A good knowledge of the various dancing figures is the key to remembering and correctly performing modern sequence dances. Dances can be stored in the memory as series of dancing figures; new dances can be picked up by translating the steps into figures — this is the method used by the experts. The problem for the aspiring sequence dancer is to convert what he sees in the dancing sessions into the appropriate dancing terms. The main burden of this book is to present the various dancing figures in such a way as to make this task easier. Emphasis is placed on the similarities between the movements used in the various dances to help the learning process.

Useful addresses

1. North Star Publishers, P.O. Box 20, Otley, West Yorkshire, LS21 2SA. (Dance script services; publisher of "Sequence Dancing World".)

2. Brockbank Lane Sequence Script Service, 1a Rodwell Avenue, Weymouth, Dorset, DT4 8UY.

3. The Dave Bullen Script Service, 24 Lyndhurst Road, Birkdale, Southport, PR8 4JT.

4. Northern Dance Services, 20 Commercial Street, Shipley, West Yorkshire, BD18 3SP. (Dance records and dance scripts.) 01274 586829

CHAPTER 3

A NEW CLASSIFICATION OF DANCING FIGURES

Standard Figures

Dancing figures are groups of steps ranging in size from the 1 step of the Reverse Pivot in the quickstep to the 30 steps of the Turkish Towel in the cha cha cha. Standard figures for a particular dance have been selected by ballroom dancing experts as being the best for general usefulness, style of performance and teaching purposes.

The old-time waltz, gavotte and two-step have standard figures derived from ballet in which the feet are placed at an angle to one another - possibly a dozen figures altogether. Swings, saunters and blues have really no standard figures of their own. Walks, points, twinkles, solo turns and rotary chasses are used in the sequences, together with standard figures from modern ballroom dances.

Dances in the modern section have some 20 main standard figures each compared with about 15 standard figures each for the Latin-American. Allowing for some figures being used in more than one dance this makes round about 150 standard figures to provide the basis of the sequences used in modern sequence dancing. In addition there are movements called variations used by advanced ballroom dancers and some special figures peculiar to the sequence dances themselves.

Dancing Manuals

Most books relevant to sequence dancing are written for ballroom dancers. Each dance with its special figures is treated in turn. A typical text for examination students

13

has 20-30 charts of figures for the quickstep giving positions of feet, footwork, alignment, amount of turn, rise and fall, CBM, sway and rhythm. Figures to precede and follow the movement are listed with suitable explanatory notes. This is fine for the advanced sequence dancer who has a good grasp of the figures and can use the charts to correct small errors in his technique. Such books are much less satisfactory for the beginner to modern sequence. There is too much detail, the naming of the figures is confusing and the range of dances and figures is restricted. There is little emphasis on similarities between figures in different dances as this is not important to the ballroom dancer who aims to perform a limited number of figures in a small range of dances with great style and elegance. The explanatory notes refer to ballroom dancing technique rather than modern sequence and there is no treatment of saunters, blues and swings.

An introductory book for the aspiring sequence dancer ought really to cover a wide range of figures in the various dances with sufficient detail to make them understandable without the text being too long and thus too expensive. The solution adopted here is to omit some of the details of style and technique since these are best dealt with by the dancing teacher at the group sessions. In addition more figures are covered by grouping similar steps together – this also helps the memory by bringing more order and reason into the process. If the underlying shape of the figure can be pictured in the mind, the music will help with the timing of the steps. Once the dancer is moving with some ease more attention can then be directed to the finer points of performance.

To the beginner the various dances in the modern sequence range seem very different in atmosphere – as, indeed, they are. The quickstep is lively, the rumba sensual and the foxtrot slow and elegant. It may be, however, that

the essential differences are in playing speed and rhythm
rather than the shapes of the dancing figures.   Some
evidence for this is set out in the following section.

Similarities Between Dances

As a change, sequence dances are sometimes played to
different rhythms.

Sequence Dance	Alternative Rhythm
Rumba Rosalie	Jive
Sindy Swing	Cha Cha Cha
Mayfair Quickstep	Samba
Tango Serida	Viennese Waltz

The dancers seem to move round comfortably enough in the
alternative styles suggesting that the dances differ more
in tempo and accentuation of beats rather than order of
steps.

In most old-time sequence dances there are bars of
waltzing despite the differences in time signatures:
3/4 for the waltz, 4/4 for the gavotte and 6/8 for the
two-step.

Several figures, such as the open telemark, whisk,
reverse pivot and outside spin, are common to the waltz,
quickstep, foxtrot and tango.   Many of the figures seem
to transfer readily from one dance to another - chasses
in the waltz, contra check and zig-zag in the tango.

All in all a classification of dancing figures by order
of foot movements seemed to have some merit.   This idea
is developed in the following chapters.

CHAPTER 4

ABBREVIATIONS AND TECHNICAL TERMS

Introduction

This chapter is really a reference section for the remainder of the book: it might well be skipped over in the preliminary reading. The standard figures use a kind of ballroom shorthand which is soon picked up by studying the list of abbreviations.

Part of a dance script is looked at in some detail to make clearer the relation between steps, figures and the complete script.

General Movement Round The Ballroom

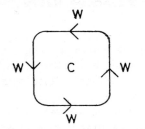

Direction of the arrows is the normal anticlockwise movement called <u>along the line of dance</u> (along LOD).
The reverse direction is <u>against line of dance.</u>

Direction of Steps (not related to position in ballroom)

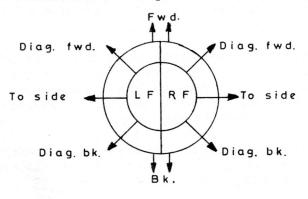

C	Centre
W	Wall
LF	Left foot
RF	Right foot
fwd	forward
bk	backward
diag	diagonal

Abbreviations Used

acr	..	across	PO	..	partner outside
ag, agst		against	posn	..	position
bhd	..	behind	prep(g)		prepare(ing)
bk(g)	.	back (backing)	PP	..	promenade position
br(g)	.	bring (bringing)	prom	..	promenade
cv(g)	.	curve (curving)	ptg	..	pointing
C	..	centre	ptnr	..	partner
diag	..	diagonal(ly)	Q	..	quick
DC	..	diagonal to centre	R	..	right
DW	..	diagonal to wall	RF	..	right foot
fcg	..	facing	RH	..	right hand
fwd	..	forward	S	..	slow
ldg	..	leading	shldr	.	shoulder
L	..	left	s-by-s	.	side-by-side
LF	..	left foot	sltly	.	slightly
LH	..	left hand	sq	..	square
LOD	..	line of dance	ss	..	small step
mvg	..	moving	trans	.	transfer
opp	..	opposite	twds	..	towards
OP	..	outside partner	ww	..	without weight

CBM: Contrary Body Movement - Turning the opposite hip and shoulder to the direction of the step being taken, e.g. as left foot moves forward, so do right hip and right shoulder.

CBMP: Contrary Body Movement Position The foot is placed on or across the line of the stationary foot. It gives a similar appearance to CBM without moving the body.

PP: Promenade Position - The partners are in a V-shaped opened-out position with the man's right side near the lady's left side. Fall-away position is promenade position with the partners moving backwards. In Counter Promenade Position (CPP) the man's and lady's positions are interchanged.

Typical Dance Script

QUATRO QUICKSTEP   (First 8 bars)   Tempo 48 b.p.m.

Graham Crookes and Doreen Wareing, ISDC 1991, Ballroom Hold, Man facing DC, Lady opposite unless stated.

1-3 REVERSE TURN, PROGRESSIVE CHASSE, 1-4 NATURAL TURN

	LF fwd DC	S
BAR 1	Side RF bkg DW	Q
	Close LF to RF bkg LOD	Q
	RF bk DC	S
BAR 2	Side LF ptg DW	Q
	Close RF to LF fcg DW	Q
	Side LF DW	S
BAR 3	RF fwd in CBMP OP	S
	Side LF bkg DC	Q
BAR 4	Close RF to LF bkg LOD	Q
	Side LF and sltly bk	S

DOUBLE BACK LOCK, TIPPLE CHASSE, LEFT SIDE LOCK

	RF bk in CBMP, R shldr ldg, bkg DW	Q
	Cross LF in front of RF	Q
BAR 5	RF bk in CBMP, R shldr ldg	Q
	Cross LF in front of RF	Q
	RF diag bk	S
BAR 6	LF bk, start turning R	S
	Side RF fcg C	Q
BAR 7	Close LF to RF	Q
	Side RF DC preparing to step OP on L	S
	LF fwd in CBMP OP on L	Q
BAR 8	Cross RF bhd LF	Q
	LF fwd in CBMP OP on L	S

In the first quarter of the dance there are 11 steps:-

 6 Quick (Q) steps (one beat)
 5 Slow (S) steps (two beats)

These make up the 16 beats - 4 in each bar. It is not always clear where the various dancing figures start and finish and sometimes figures have steps left out. In this example:-

1-3 REVERSE TURN   BAR 1 (3 steps)

PROGRESSIVE CHASSE   BAR 2 and first step of BAR 3
                             (4 steps)

1-4 NATURAL TURN   Second step of BAR 3 and BAR 4
                             (4 steps)

Partner's Steps

Man's steps are given in the script and lady's are said to be opposite. This means that as the man's left foot moves forward the lady's right foot moves backwards and so on. Where lady's steps are not opposite they are written in brackets after the man's steps. Some scripts give the lady's steps in full on a separate page. In this case the dancing figures may differ slightly as she is usually moving in the opposite direction to the man.

ISDC 1991

Winner of the Modern Section of the competition held by the International Sequence Dance Circle (Llandudno, September 1991).

48 b.p.m.

Recommended playing speed (tempo) is 48 bars per minute.

19

Alignments In The Script

The abbreviations DC, DW in the script refer to the
alignment. In modern sequence dancing this refers to the
direction in which the foot is pointing in relation to
the line of dance.   (In some old-time dances alignment
refers to the position of the body rather than the foot.)
If the foot and the body are in line the terms facing
(fcg) and backing (bkg) are used; if not, the foot is
said to be pointing (ptg).

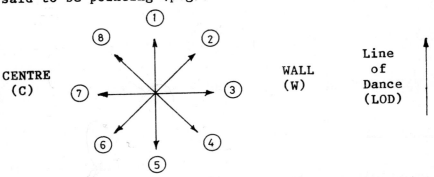

CENTRE
(C)

WALL
(W)

Line
of
Dance
(LOD)

When about to move forwards in direction	When about to move backwards against the direction
1. Facing LOD	1. Backing agst LOD
2. Facing DW	2. Backing DC agst LOD
3. Facing W	3. Backing C
4. Facing DW agst LOD	4. Backing DC
5. Facing agst LOD	5. Backing LOD
6. Facing DC agst LOD	6. Backing DW
7. Facing C	7. Backing W
8. Facing DC	8. Backing DW agst LOD

Dance scripts are useful for learning and memorising dances and for sorting out difficulties with particular steps. Some dancers arrange to have the scripts sent to them as soon as the new dances appear. They are by no means essential for the average sequence dancer and a good knowledge of dancing figures is far more useful.

Dancing Turns

Figures involving turns are among the most complex likely to be encountered in modern sequence dancing. Steps for man and lady are often quite different at different stages of the turn. These problems increase as the angle of turn gets larger – for turns less than one quarter the lady's steps are often just the mirror image of the man's steps. Problems with turns arise from a number of factors – need to maintain body contact for leading purposes, line and appearance to onlookers, comfort in performance, etc. There is also a physical factor relating to the distance travelled during the turn referred to as being on the inside or outside of a turn (see later).

Amount of Turn

The amount of turn is measured by the angle between the positions of the <u>feet</u> when moving from one step to another (not the position of the body as in old-time dancing).

A <u>clockwise turn</u> to the <u>right</u> is called a <u>natural turn</u>; an <u>anticlockwise</u> turn to the <u>left</u> is a <u>reverse turn</u>. Multiples of 1/8 of a turn are used. The amount of turn relates to the angle between the feet - it has nothing to do with the distance travelled in moving from one step to another.

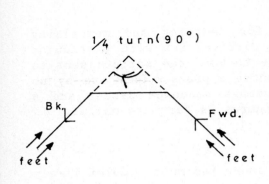

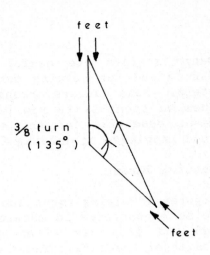

Quarter turn to right
(Natural)

Reverse Turn (to left)
(3/8 turn)

This is the main method of indicating the amount of turn used in this text.

In dance scripts the usual way of specifying the amount of turn is by the change in alignment of the feet. In the example of the reverse turn above the initial alignment is Facing diagonal to centre (fcg DC); the final alignment is Backing line of dance (bk LOD). In charts of figures set out in ballroom manuals, both methods are used.

Reverse Turn			
Step	Positions of Feet	Alignment	Amount of Turn
1	LF fwd	Facing DC	Start to turn L on 1
2	RF to side	Backing DW	1/4 between 1 and 2
3	LF closes to RF	Backing LOD	1/8 between 2 and 3

The Inside and Outside of a Turn

In a dancing turn the partner moving <u>forward</u> has to cover a greater distance in consequence of being on the <u>outside</u> of the turn. In 1-3 of the Waltz Reverse Turn the man is on the outside and the lady on the inside.

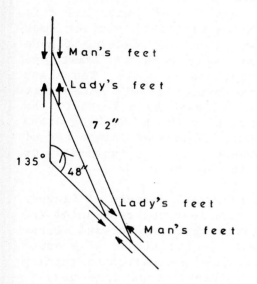

Two Strides	
Man 72"	Lady 48"

Man's Steps (Lady's opposite)	
1. LF fwd	⅜
2. RF to side	turn
3. LF closes to RF	to L

Waltz Reverse Turn

On the outside of the turn, the foot swivels on the second step and the turning takes place over all three steps. On the inside, the lady's turn takes place over the first two steps, although the body completes the turn on the third step.

Remember:-

(a) Moving forward - outside of a turn. Turn more slowly and travel further. Stretch the side step.

(b) Moving backward - inside of a turn. Turn more sharply and travel less.

23

CHAPTER 5

WALKS, THREE-STEPS, CHANGES AND HESITATIONS

Forward and Backward Walks

In modern sequence the man usually starts with his left foot moving forward (Lakeside Rumba (1991) - right foot moving backward). This means that any dancing figure starting with the right foot will need at least one preliminary step to change the leading foot. The Alana Foxtrot (1967) and the Sahara Foxtrot (1991) both start with a left foot forward step followed by a feather; the Margie Quickstep (1990) starts with a walking step followed by a natural pivot turn. The most common way of changing the leading foot, however, is by a three-step or change as it is often called in the waltz.

Forward walking steps are an important feature of tangos, saunters, blues and swings. Each four-bar section of the Kingfisher Saunter (1990) starts with two forward steps. Walks are slow steps often used in the middle of a dance to give time for readjustment after a complicated turning figure. In foxtrots the walking steps are usually included in the foxtrot figures.

Although the forward walk is the simplest of all dancing figures this does not mean that it is easy to perform well. It has been said that the basis of good dancing is a sound technique for the forward and backward walks. Different styles of walk are needed for the different dances:-

Foxtrot	-	Long, slow gliding steps (saunter - slower still);
Quickstep	-	Short and lively movements;
Blues	-	A "lilting" walk;
Samba, Jive	-	A "bouncy" action;

24

Tango   -   Firm, deliberate steps, knees slightly
                bent;
Two-Step   -   A marching military walk.

There is plenty of scope for the dancing teacher here!

Backward walks are more difficult to perform than the modified walking action of the forward steps. It is not easy to maintain poise and balance whilst taking a long enough backward step.

The Three-Step

The three-step starting with the right foot is possibly the most important figure in the slow foxtrot. Just as the chasse is used in the quickstep and waltz to change the rhythm so does the Quick, Quick, Slow of the three-step give the foxtrot its special characteristics.

Three-Step		Timing	
Man's Steps	Lady's Steps	Foxtrot	Others
1. RF fwd	1. LF bk	Q	S
2. LF fwd	2. RF bk	Q	S
3. RF fwd	3. LF bk	S	S

The three-step may be started with the left foot or taken in a backward direction, e.g. bar 14 of the Melody Foxtrot (1963). The Eva Three-Step (1904) consists largely of three-steps followed by a point, taken in forward, backward and sideways directions.

The Feather Step

The feather step consists of a slow walking step followed by a three-step starting with the left foot. It is a most elegant step in which the man steps outside the lady on the second quick step and then moves back in line.

Feather Step		Timing
Man's Steps	Lady's Steps	
1. RF fwd	1. LF bk	S
2. LF fwd L shldr lead preparing to step OP	2. RF bk R shldr lead	Q
3. RF fwd in CBMP OP	3. LF bk in CBMP	Q
4. LF fwd partner square	4. RF bk partner square	S

Many turns and figures have a "feather ending" or "feather finish" consisting of the last 3 steps of the feather. The feather can be taken from promenade position (Tempro Foxtrot (1992)).

"Feather" generally implies some movement outside the partner.

The Progressive Side Step

This is a forward three-step in which the second step is taken sideways; it should curve to the left. It is a standard figure in the tango and involves a quickening of the tango walk.

Progressive Side Step		Timing
Man's Steps	**Lady's Steps**	
1. LF fwd in CBMP	1. RF bk in CBMP	Q
2. RF to side, sltly bk	2. LF to side, sltly fwd	Q
3. LF fwd in CBMP	3. RF bk in CBMP	S

The progressive side step reverse turn is the above figure with a strong turn to the left followed by a step forward with the right foot, often taken against the line of dance (Glendale Tango (1991)).

Curved (Curving) Three-Steps and Feathers

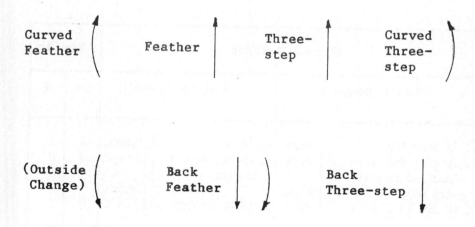

Curved Feather   Feather   Three-step   Curved Three-step

(Outside Change)   Back Feather   Back Three-step

Curved (Curving) Three-Step

This is a three-step with up to 1/4 turn to the <u>left</u>. In the Sahara Foxtrot (1991) there is a curving three-step in which the man has to turn the lady and move in line; this figure requires good technique. The Westlynn Waltz (1990) has a curved three-step in which the man walks round the lady on the left side.

The Saga Waltz (1988) has 3 backward curving walks.

Curved and Back Feathers

A <u>curved feather</u> consists of the first 3 steps of the feather curving up to 1/4 turn to the <u>right</u>. It is usually followed by a backward movement. Examples are:-

Sahara Foxtrot (1991) followed by an open impetus turn;
Nevada Foxtrot (1990) followed by a curved back feather;
Blue Lace Waltz (1991) followed by an outside change.

Curved Feather		Timing	
Man's Steps	Lady's Steps	F	W

1. RF diag fwd ⎤ ⅛turn
2. LF diag fwd, L shldr ⎦ to R
   leading, prep to
   step OP ⎤ ⅛turn
3. RF fwd in CBMP OP ⎦ to R
	1. LF bk ⎤ ⅛turn
	2. RF bk, R shldr ⎦ to R
	   leading
	                    ⎤ ⅛turn
	3. LF bk in CBMP ss ⎦ to R
		S
		Q
		
		Q
			S
			S
			
			S

F = Foxtrot/W = Waltz

A <u>back feather</u> occurs in the April Foxtrot (1992).

Back Feather		Timing
Man's Steps	**Lady's Steps**	
1. LF bk in CBMP	1. RF fwd in CBMP OP	S
2. RF bk, R shldr leading	2. LF fwd, L shldr leading	Q
3. LF bk in CBMP	3. RF fwd in CBMP OP	Q

A <u>curved back feather</u> has a 1/8 turn to the right over the 3 steps (Nevada Foxtrot (1990)).

Forward and Backward Closed Changes

The forward closed changes are among the oldest of the dancing figures. In the early days of the waltz they were used to change from natural to reverse turns and vice versa. The modern waltz is sometimes called the "diagonal" waltz and these changes are three-steps with a triangular pattern; the feet are closed on the last step. Many social dancers replace these changes with forward walks and lose the opportunity of performing a very graceful waltz figure.

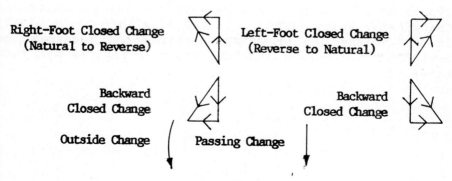

Right-Foot Closed Change (Natural to Reverse)   Left-Foot Closed Change (Reverse to Natural)

Backward Closed Change   Backward Closed Change

Outside Change   Passing Change

Right Foot Closed Change (Natural to Reverse)	Left-Foot Closed Change (Reverse to Natural)	Timing
Man's Steps	Man's Steps	
1. RF fwd	1. LF fwd	S
2. LF to side, sltly fwd	2. RF to side, sltly fwd	S
3. RF closes to LF	3. LF closes to RF	S

(Lady's steps opposite)

Some turns finish with a backward closed change – this is called a "closed finish".

Combining a forward closed change with the appropriate backward closed change makes a waltz square (see later).

The Outside Change

The outside change is a standard figure in the waltz; it involves a 1/4 turn to the left without the feet being closed at any stage. It occurs in the Waltz Babette and Charminster Waltz (1989). In the Blue Lace Waltz (1991) it is finished in promenade position and reverses the action of the curved feather; these 2 figures are then repeated.

Outside Change	Outside Change to PP	Timing
Man's Steps	**Man's Steps**	
1. LF bk in CBMP	1. Partner on right side	S
2. RF bk ⎤ ¼ turn	2. Partner turned square	S
3. LF to side, ⎦ to sltly fwd L	3. In promenade position	S

(Lady's steps opposite)

Passing Changes

These are backward three-steps with a 1/8 turn. They are "open" figures like the outside change – the feet pass one another instead of closing, Westgate Waltz (1987), Stardust Waltz (1989).

Change of Direction

Change of Direction		Timing
Man's Steps	**Lady's Steps**	
1. LF fwd ⎤ ¼ turn to L	1. RF bk ⎤ ¼ turn to L	S
2. RF diag fwd, R shldr leading LF closes to RF, sltly fwd ww ⎦	2. LF diag bk L shldr ldg RF closes to LF, sltly bk ww ⎦	S
3. LF fwd in CBMP	3. RF bk in CBMP	S

31

The change of direction is a standard figure in foxtrots. It often starts with the last step of the feather (Sahara Foxtrot (1991)). The Chandella Quickstep (1990) ends with a type of change of direction.

Hesitations

Hesitations involve a step in which one foot closes to the other without weight. There is a feeling of waiting before moving off with this same foot.

The <u>Hesitation Change</u> is a rapid method of moving from 1 to 3 of the natural turn to 1 to 3 of the reverse turn. After the natural turn steps, the man steps back with his left foot and slowly pulls his right foot towards it. After a slight hesitation he goes into the reverse turn (Woodside Waltz, Eivona Quickstep).

The Drag Hesitation

In the waltz this figure is often followed by a back lock (Rose Lane Waltz, Waltz Louise (1989)). It is used in the April Foxtrot (1992).

Drag Hesitation		Timing	
Man's Steps	Lady's Steps	W	F
1. LF fwd ⎤¼ turn	1. RF bk ⎤¼ turn	S	S
2. RF to side⎦ to L	2. LF to side⎦ to L	S	Q
3. LF closes ⎤⅛turn	3. RF closes ⎤⅛turn	S	Q
to RF ww ⎦ to L	to LF ww ⎦ to L		

W = Waltz/F = Foxtrot

32

The Twinkle

Quick and slow twinkles are standard figures in social
rhythm dancing. The twinkle is used in saunters, swings,
tangos and other types of sequence dance. It is a type
of change step like the chasse and the three-step —
leaving out a twinkle will leave the dancer on the wrong
leading foot. Twinkles may be started with either foot
or taken forwards or backwards.

Right Forward Twinkle		Timing	
Man's Steps	Lady's Steps		
1. RF fwd	1. LF bk	Q	S
2. LF closes to RF	2. RF closes to LF	Q	S
3. RF bk	3. LF fwd	S	S

Adding a fourth step closing the feet together gives the
closed twinkle. The Columbine Saunter (1991) ends with a
left forward closed twinkle, timed Q, Q, Q, Q. The
Cheney Blues (1992) has a backward twinkle with close
whilst the lady does circling walks; this is repeated
with the roles reversed.

CHAPTER 6

CHECKS, ROCKS AND HOVERS

Reversing Movements

A check usually involves a change in direction from a
forward to a backward movement with the weight being
replaced to the back foot. The Harlequin Foxtrot (1990)
has a checked feather, the Alana Foxtrot (1967) has a
checked weave in bars 3 and 4. The first step in the
basic movement of rumba and cha cha cha is sometimes
described as a checked forward walk.

Rocks are a type of check in which the forward and
backward movement is usually repeated. The rock should
be made with the body without the feet being too firmly
planted. Rock turns are common in tangos.

In hovers the checking action is carried out with a
floating movement, the weight being transferred from one
foot to the other rising on the toes. Hovers are
graceful figures used in slower dances such as the waltz
and foxtrot.

The cucaracha (beetle-crusher) used in the rumba has a
very different action from the hover. It is a pressure
step consisting of three steps, the feet being closed on
the third step. It is often taken sideways with part
weight (1. LF to side with part wt; 2. Replace wt to RF;
3. Close LF to RF).

The lunge, as the name implies, is a long step made
longer by bending the knee of the other leg. The same
foot lunge is found in many sequence dances:- Kingfisher
Saunter (1990), April Foxtrot (1992), Hadrian's Waltz
(1992). The man's foot moves sideways whilst the lady's
same foot moves backwards.

34

Some reversing movements do not involve a transfer of weight and two steps are taken with the same foot. A preliminary step is followed by a <u>point</u> (Sindy Swing (1984)) or a <u>flick</u> (Sharron Swing (1990)) or a <u>swing</u> in low aerial position (Singapore Swing (1992)).

Contra Checks

Contra checks and whisks are often used in waltzes and foxtrots to move in and out of promenade position to give variety. The Bellerby Waltz (1991) starts with a travelling contra check; the Tempro Foxtrot (1992) starts with a whisk and feather ending. The progressive and promenade links are figures used in the tango for this purpose.

The <u>contra check</u> is a standard figure in the waltz (Emmerdale Waltz, Apple Blossom Waltz (1992)). It is also used in the tango with a SQQ timing (Tango Solair (1970), Tango Negro (1992)).

Contra Check		Waltz Timing
Man's Steps	**Lady's Steps**	
1. LF fwd in CBMP	1. RF bk in CBMP	S
2. Replace wt to RF	2. Replace wt to LF	S
3. LF to side in PP	3. RF to side in PP	S

In making the first step some weight should be retained on the right foot. The body should turn towards the left on the first step and to the right on the second step. This figure is taken with the partner in line ("contra" means "against").

35

The travelling contra check is a contra check with the second step replaced by the right foot taking a small step to the side and slightly forward; the body is turned slightly to the right (Claudia's Waltz (1991), Denverdale Waltz (1992)).

Outside Checks

Checks outside the partner followed by a chasse or side step are found in many sequence dances - see Chapter 8 (Rumba and Cha Cha Cha figures).

The chair is a sort of inside check.

The Chair	Timing	
Man's Steps (Lady's steps opposite)	F	W
1. LF to side in PP along LOD	Q	S
2. RF fwd and across in PP/CBMP, knees flexed	S	S
3. Replace wt to LF	Q	S

F = Foxtrot/W = Waltz

The Glenroy Foxtrot, Carousel Saunter (1991), Blue Dawn Waltz (1991) have chairs with different timings. The fencing line is a type of chair in which the partners' joined hands are forward and the other arms held out backwards in fencing position (Rumba One, Renaissance Rumba (1992), Commador Cha Cha Cha (1992)).

Progressive and Promenade Links

The progressive link is used in the tango instead of the travelling contra check to move into promenade position. It consists of the first two steps of the progressive side step with the lady being turned into promenade position.

Progressive Link		Timing
Man's Steps	**Lady's steps**	
1. LF fwd in CBMP	1. RF bk in CBMP] ¼ turn to R	Q
2. RF to side, sltly bk in PP, body turns to R	2. LF to side and sltly bk in PP	Q

This figure has become more popular with the introduction of the more staccato action of the modern tango. It is used in the Glendale and Torque Tangos (1991).

The promenade link is used to change from a promenade figure into a forward figure such as a four-step or progressive side step.

Promenade Link		Timing
Man's Steps	**Lady's steps**	
1. LF to side in PP	1. RF to side in PP	S
2. RF fwd & across in CBMP and PP	2. LF fwd & across in CBMP and PP] ¼ turn to L	Q
3. LF to side ww (small step)	3. RF to side ww (small step)	Q

The promenade link is found in the Tango Debonaire (1990) and Tango Negro (1992).

37

Rocks

Open rocks have the legs apart, closed rocks have the
legs in CBMP. They may start with either foot and be
taken backward or forward or to the side. The rock is
often taken with the man moving backwards against the
line of dance (see following figure).

Left Foot (Open) Rock	Tango Timing
Man's Steps (Lady's steps opposite)	
1. LF bk, L shldr leading	Q
2. Transfer wt fwd to RF, R shldr leading	Q
3. LF bk, L shldr leading (small step)	S

Rocks are found in the Renaissance Rumba (1992), Telecon
Tango (1992), Sacha Swing (1991).

The Natural Rock Turn

Natural Rock Turn				Timing
Man's Steps		Lady's steps		
1. RF fwd, R shldr ldg	¼	1. LF bk, L shldr ldg	¼	S
2. LF to side, sltly bk	turn	2. RF fwd, sltly to R	turn	Q
3. Transfer wt fwd to RF, R shldr leading	to R	3. LF bk, sltly to L, L shldr leading	to R	Q
4. LF bk, L shldr leading ss		4. RF fwd, R shldr leading ss		S
5. RF bk in CBMP	¼ turn	5. LF fwd in CBMP	¼ turn	Q
6. LF to side, sltly fwd	to L	6. RF to side, sltly bk	to L	Q
7. RF closes to RF, sltly bk		7. LF closes to RF, sltly fwd		S

The natural rock turn is a forward rock turned to the right with a closed finish (steps 5, 6, 7).

A natural rock turn is used in the Taurus Tango (1991); a reverse rock turn appears in the Karen Foxtrot (1959).

Hovers

Hovers are standard figures in the slow foxtrot (Hover Cross, Hover Feather and Hover Telemark turns). They are often used in the waltz and sometimes in swings, blues and saunters. There are many types of hovers and they are often described rather loosely in the sequences – hover, hover from PP and promenade hover used for the same set of steps. Simple forward hovers are hardly detectable when danced by many sequence dancers. Turning hovers of various kinds are found in the Grosvenor Foxtrot (1991), White Heather Foxtrot (1991) and Claudia's Waltz (1991). These hovers usually involve a turning of the body first in one direction and then the other with relatively little foot movement – they are popular and well executed by most sequence dancers.

Forward Hover	– Sacha Swing	(1991)
	– Centenary Saunter	(1992)
Back Hover	– Apple Blossom Waltz	(1992)
Closed Hover	– Caribbean Foxtrot	(1986)
Hover Cross	– Fortuna Foxtrot	(1990)
	– Nicola Foxtrot	(1991)
Hover Telemark	– Nevada Foxtrot	(1990)
Travelling Hover	– Blue Dawn Waltz	(1991)
Hover Corte	– Caribbean Foxtrot	(1986)
	– Hadrian's Waltz	(1992)

CHAPTER 7

WHISKS, WINGS AND ZIG-ZAGS

The Whisk

The forward whisk is essentially a triangular movement for the man ending with feet crossed; the lady turns into promenade position.

(Forward) Whisk		Timing	
Man's Steps	**Lady's Steps**	**W**	**F**
1. LF fwd	1. RF bk ⎤ ¼ turn	S	S
2. RF to side, sltly fwd	2. LF diag bk ⎦ to R	S	Q
3. LF crosses behind RF, turning lady into PP	3. RF crosses bhd LF in PP	S	Q

W = Waltz/F = Foxtrot

The forward whisk is often followed by a wing, e.g. Bluebird Waltz, Harlequin Foxtrot (1990). Several foxtrots start with a forward whisk followed by a feather from promenade position (White Heather Foxtrot (1991), Tempro Foxtrot (1992)).

The Left Whisk

In this figure the man steps forward and across with the right foot. The lady usually does a <u>twist turn</u> consisting of four quick steps twisting the man to the right and allowing his feet to uncross (Bellerby Waltz (1991), Hadrian's Waltz (1992)).

Left Whisk				Waltz Timing
Man's Steps		**Lady's Steps**		
1. RF fwd and across in CBMP and PP		1. LF fwd and across in CBMP and PP	⌉ ¼ turn to L	S
2. LF to side and sltly fwd	⌉ Body turns	2. RF to side and sltly bk	⌋ ⌉ ⅛ turn to L	S
3. RF crosses bhd LF	⌋ L	3. LF bk in CBMP	⌋	S

Back Whisk

Back Whisk				Timing
Man's Steps		**Lady's Steps**		
1. LF bk in CBMP		1. RF fwd in CBMP OP	⌉ ⅛ turn to R	S
2. RF diag bk		2. LF to side	⌋	S
3. LF crosses bhd RF in PP		3. RF crosses bhd LF in PP	⌉ ⅛ turn to R	S

The Westlynn Waltz (1990) has a back whisk followed by a
wing; in the Wetheral Waltz (1990) it is followed by a
chasse from promenade position.

Fallaway Whisk

This is a back whisk with a turn to the right by the man also and a correspondingly larger turn by the lady.

Fallaway Whisk		Timing
Man's Steps	**Lady's Steps**	

1. LF bk ⎤ ⅜ turn
2. RF to side, ⎥ to R
   sltly bk ⎦
3. LF crosses
   loosely bhd
   RF in fallaway
	1. RF fwd ⎤ ⅜ turn
	2. LF to side ⎦ to R
	
	3. RF crosses ⎤
	   loosely bhd ⎥ ¼ turn
	   LF in fallaway⎦ to R
		S
		S
		
		S

The Emmerdale Waltz has a Fallaway Whisk followed by a Wing.

The Wing

In the wing the man makes a small turn to the left whilst the lady walks round him to his left side.

The Wing		Timing Waltz
Man's Steps	**Lady's Steps**	

1. RF fwd and across
   in CBMP and PP
2. LF starts to close ⎤ Body
   to RF ⎥ turns
3. LF closes to RF ww ⎦ to L
	1. LF fwd in CBMP ⎤ ⅛
	   and PP ⎥ turn
	2. RF fwd preparing ⎦ to L
	   to step OP ⎤
	3. LF fwd in CBMP OP ⎥ ¼ turn
	   on partner's L side⎦ to L
		S
		
		S
		
		S

The Wing is often followed by the open telemark (Woodside Waltz, Emmerdale Waltz, Apple Blossom Waltz (1992)).

42

The Closed Wing

This figure is similar to the normal wing but the partners are square to each other. The lady moves across the man from his right hand side to his left hand side (Blue Lace Waltz (1991)).

Closed Wing		Timing
Man's Steps	Lady's Steps	Waltz
1. RF fwd in CBMP OP	1. LF bk in CBMP	S
2. LF starts to close to RF	2. RF to side, sltly bk ss	S
3. LF closes to RF ww	3. LF fwd in CBMP OP on partner's L side	S

Closed wings with various timings occur in the Tango Las Vegas, Cerise Saunter (1992) and April Foxtrot (1992).

Reverse and Natural Zig-Zag

The (reverse) zig-zag has 1/4 turn to L; 1/4 turn to R. The natural zig-zag has up to 1/4 turn to R; 1/4 turn to L.

Both zig-zags are very popular and the amount of turn and timing are often modified to suit the particular dance.

The (Reverse) Zig-Zag				Quickstep
Man's Steps		Lady's Steps		Timing
1. LF fwd	⌉ ¼ turn	1. RF bk	⌉ ¼ turn	S
2. RF to side ss	⌋ to L	2. LF closes to RF (heel turn)	⌋ to L	S
3. LF bk in CBMP PO	⌉	3. RF fwd in CBMP OP	⌉	S
4. Pull RF bk to LF turning on heel of LF	¼ turn to R	4. LF to side	¼ turn to R	S
5. LF fwd brushing past RF	⌋	5. RF bk brushing past LF	⌋	S

The (reverse) zig-zag is used in the Woodspring Quickstep (1988), Chandella Quickstep (1990), Saunter Together (1975), Kingfisher Saunter (1990), Tango Leanne (1992) and Fiesta Cha Cha Cha.

The _natural zig-zag_ is a basic figure in the slow foxtrot; it is often taken from promenade position.

Natural Zig-Zag from Promenade Position		Timing
Man's Steps	**Lady's Steps**	
1. RF fwd and across in CBMP and PP ⌉ ⅛ turn	1. LF fwd and across in CBMP and PP	S S
2. LF to side ⌋ to R	2. RF diag fwd preparing to step OP	Q S
3. RF bk in CBMP ⌉ ⅛ turn	3. LF fwd in CBMP OP ⌉ ⅛ turn on partner's side ⌋ to L	Q S
4. LF to side, sltly fwd ⌋ to L	4. RF to side ⌉ ⅛ turn	Q S
5. RF fwd in CBMP OP	5. LF bk in CBMP ⌋ to L	Q S

Harlequin Foxtrot (1990), Sharron Swing (1990), Centenary Saunter (1992), Blue Lace Waltz (1991), Cameron Quickstep. Various timings are used.

The Running Zig-Zag (and Running Finish)

This quickstep figure consists of the first two steps of the zig-zag followed by the running finish.

The Idaho Foxtrot (1959) has a reverse running zig-zag; the Claymore Cha Cha Cha (1991) has both natural and reverse running zig-zags.

The _running finish_ is used in many sequence quicksteps. In the Quando Quickstep and Roxy Quickstep (1991) it follows a back lock and leads into a natural spin turn. In the Florentine Quickstep (1992), the alternative timing SQQS is used.

Running Zig-Zag (Reverse)				Quickstep Timing
	Man's Steps		**Lady's Steps**	

Zig-Zag	1. LF fwd ¼ turn
	2. RF to side, to L
	    sltly bk ss
			1. RF bk ¼ turn
			2. LF closes to RF to L
			    (heel turn)
				S
				S

Run.
Fin.
	3. LF bk in CBMP
	    ldg ptnr outside ¼ turn
	4. RF to side, to R
	5. LF diag fwd
	    prepg to step OP
	6. RF fwd in CBMP OP
			3. RF fwd in CBMP OP
			        ¼ turn
			4. LF to side, to R
			5. RF diag bk
			
			6. LF bk in CBMP PO
				Q
				
				Q
				S
				
				S

The Four-Step

This is a standard figure in the tango. It is a square figure rather like a forward closed twinkle with more sideways movement.

Tango Four-Step		Tango Timing
Man's Steps	**Lady's Steps**	

1. LF fwd in CBMP
2. RF to side,
    sltly bk
3. LF bk in CBMP
4. RF closes to LF,
    sltly bk in PP
	1. RF bk in CBMP
	2. LF to side,
	    sltly fwd
	3. RF fwd in CBMP OP ⎤
	          ¼ turn
	4. LF closes to RF, to R
	    sltly bk in PP ⎦
		Q
		Q
		
		Q
		Q

Four-steps are found in the Tango Debonaire (1990), Carousel Saunter (1991) and Cheney Blues (1992).

A turning four-step has a turn to the left (Saunter Sateen (1991), Tango Leanne (1992)). It is very similar to steps 1 to 4 of the reverse zig-zag.

45

CHAPTER 8

CHASSÉS AND LOCK STEPS

A <u>chassé</u> (chasing step) consists essentially of three steps counted Quick, Quick, Slow with the feet being closed on the second step. Like the three-step of the slow foxtrot it changes the rhythm and the leading foot. Many chasses are taken in a sideways direction.

Side Chasses

Chasse to R	Chasse to L	Timing
Man's Steps	Man's Steps	
1. RF to side	1. LF to side	Q
2. LF closes to RF	2. RF closes to LF	Q
3. RF to side	3. LF to side	S
———▶ Often written as chasse RLR	◀——— Often written as chasse LRL	

(The lady does the opposite side chasse to the man.) The short form of notation for the chasse is used in some dance scripts, e.g.

<u>Anitra Cha Cha Cha</u> (Bar 1)

        Side LF to chasse LRL

<u>Cuban Swing</u> (Bar 5)

        Chasse LRL towards centre

46

Chasse figures are common in the quickstep, cha cha cha and jive. In the cha cha cha and jive the feet are only half-closed on the second step. The jive chasse has a timing of $\frac{3}{4}:\frac{1}{4}:1$ instead of $\frac{1}{2}:\frac{1}{2}:1$ (QQS) as in the other dances.

Many lock steps are alternatives to the chasse in which one foot is crossed behind the other instead of the feet being closed on the second step. Forward chasses are often replaced by lock steps.

The chasse is often preceded by a walking (slow) step and many chasses are of the form:-

$$S \quad Q \quad Q \quad S$$

Feet closed

The nature and direction of these two slow steps determine the character of the chasse dancing figure. If there is no turn within the chasse itself the lady's steps are opposite to the man's and the figures are easy to describe and execute.

Cross Chasse   **Part of Chasse Square**

Notice that the feet are always pointing in the same direction although the legs move forwards, backwards and sideways.

47

Cross Chasses

Cross Chasse to R	Timing
Man's Steps (Lady's opposite)	
1. LF fwd	S
2. RF to side	Q
3. LF closes to RF	Q

This is a triangular figure like the closed change in the waltz. It is usually followed by a step with the right foot outside the partner.

Chasse Squares

Chasse squares are common in older sequence dances. Waltz squares have similar steps but different timing (no chasse).

Clockwise Chasse Square	Timing	
Man's Steps	Chasse	Waltz
1. LF fwd	S	S
2. RF to side	Q	S
3. LF closes to RF	Q	S
4. RF bk	S	S
5. LF to side	Q	S
6. RF closes to LF	Q	S

(Lady's steps opposite

The Square Tango, Sindy Swing and Melody Foxtrot have clockwise squares; the Eugene Tango has an anticlockwise square. The Festival Glide has both types in a figure of eight. The Waltz Sincere and Sweetheart Waltz have clockwise waltz squares.

Promenade Chasses

Partners carry out the chasses moving down the line of dance in promenade position. The feet and body are diagonal to the direction of motion. The Apple Blossom Waltz (1992) has this figure in bars 2 and 13. The promenade chasse or "conversation piece" is a standard figure in social rhythm dancing.

Promenade Chasse	Timing
Man's Steps (Lady's steps opposite)	
1. RF fwd and across in CBMP and PP	S
2. LF to side and sltly fwd in PP	Q
3. RF closes to LF in PP	Q
4. LF to side and sltly fwd	S

Forward and Backward Lock Steps

A lock step is a type of chasse in which one foot is crossed behind the other instead of being closed on the third step. Lock steps are often used instead of forward and backward chasses.

Forward Lock Step	Backward Lock Step	Timing
Man's or Lady's Steps	**Man's or Lady's Steps**	
1. RF fwd in CBMP OP	1. LF bk in CBMP	S
2. LF fwd sltly to L	2. RF bk	Q
3. RF crosses bhd LF	3. LF crosses in front of RF	Q
4. LF fwd slightly to L	4. RF bk sltly to R	S

A turning back lock is a backward lock step followed by a quarter turn to the left on the following step; it often follows the natural spin turn in the waltz.

The Chandella Quickstep (1990) and Nicola Foxtrot (1991) have double forward locks whereas the Quatro Quickstep (1991) has a double backward lock. Hadrian's Waltz (1992) has a back lock and a slow lock; the slow lock step is not a chasse.

The Fishtail

This is a popular figure in sequence quicksteps; it is found also in the Singapore Swing (1992).

Fishtail		Timing
Man's Steps (Lady's steps opposite)		
Lock on opposite foot	1. RF fwd in CBMP OP	S
	2. LF crosses behind RF	Q
	3. RF fwd sltly to side, ss	Q
Lock on normal foot	4. LF fwd sltly to L	Q
	5. RF crosses behind LF	Q
	6. LF fwd sltly to L	S

The fishtail may be danced without turn or there may be 1/4 turn to the right between steps 1 and 3. There is a sway to the right on 2 and to the left on 4 which gives the fishtail its name. A back fishtail is found in the Queslett Quickstep (1992).

CHAPTER 9

SOME CHA CHA CHA AND RUMBA FIGURES

Although the cha cha cha and rumba are very different in character they have many similarities. Thus both dances are written in 4/4 time and should be started on the second beat. In many figures the cha cha cha chasse is replaced by a single slow step in the rumba. The standard rhythms of the two dances are set out below.

Bars	Cha Cha Cha					Rumba		
	2	3	4	and	1	2	3	4 1
Beat values	1	1	½	½	1	1	1	2
	Step	Step	Cha	Cha	Cha			
	S	S	Q	Q	S	Q	Q	S
				Chasse				

Notice that the slow step takes 1 beat in the cha cha cha but 2 beats in the rumba. Hence timings in this section will be given in beat values. Compare the forward basic figures for the two dances.

	Forward Basic				
	Man's Steps (Lady's steps opposite)				
	Cha Cha Cha	Beat Values	Rumba	Beat Values
Chasse LRL	1. LF fwd	1	1. LF fwd	1
	2. Replace wt to RF	1	2. Replace wt to RF	1
	3. LF to side, sltly bk	½		
	4. RF half closed to LF	½	3. LF to side	2
	5. LF to side	1		
	⅛ – ¼ turn to L		⅛ – ¼ turn to L	

The steps of the <u>back basic</u> are similar but starting with right foot back for the man followed by a RLR chasse.

51

Figures with Checks

In the checking action weight is tranferred to the leading foot and then replaced to the back foot. Figures involving a check taken outside the partner followed by a chasse or side step are found in many sequence dances. They are very common in Latin-American dances since the partners stand further apart and may indeed both check forward at the same time (see the New York).

Shoulder to Shoulder

In this figure as the man checks forward, the lady steps backward.

Shoulder to Shoulder (Man's Steps, Lady's Opposite)			Beat value	
	Cha Cha Cha	Rumba	CCC	Rumba
Check	1. RF fwd OP (R side)	1. RF fwd OP (R side)	1	1
	2. Replace wt to LF	2. Replace wt to LF	1	1
Chasse RLR	3. RF to side ⌉ ¼	turning ¼ to R	½	
	4. LF ½ closed to RF ⎟ turn	3. RF to side	½	2
	5. RF to side ⌋ to R		1	
Check	6. LF fwd OP (L side)	4. LF fwd OP (L side)	1	1
	7. Replace wt to RF	5. Replace wt to RF	1	1
Chasse LRL	8. LF to side ⌉ ¼	turning ¼ to L	½	
	9. RF ½ closed to LF ⎟ turn	6. LF to side	½	2
	10. LF to side ⌋ to L		1	

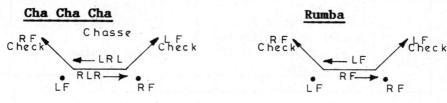

Cha Cha Cha

Rumba

Also Mayfair Quickstep (1959)   Also Westlynn Waltz (1990)
Catherine Waltz (1956)
Caribbean Foxtrot (1986)

The New York

The outside check from open promenade position (and counter promenade position) is called the New York (or New Yorker). Both partners check forward at the same time.

New York (Man's Steps)		Beat value	
Cha Cha Cha	**Rumba**	**CCC**	**Rumba**
1. RF fwd in Open PP ⎤ ⅛ turn to L	1. As in CCC ⎤ ⅛ turn to L	1	1
2. Replace wt to LF ⎤ ⅜ turn to R 3-5. Chasse RLR ⎦	2. As in CCC ⎤ ⅜ turn to R 3. LF to side ⎦	1 ½½1	1 2
6. LF fwd in Open CPP ⎤ ⅛ turn to R	4. As in CCC ⎤ ⅛ turn to R	1	1
7. Replace wt to RF ⎤ ⅜ turn to L 8-10. Chasse LRL ⎦	5. As in CCC ⎤ ⅜ turn to L 6. RF to side ⎦	1 ½½1	1 2
Lady does steps 6-10 as man does steps 1-5 and vice versa.	Lady does steps 4-6 as man does steps 1-3 and vice versa.		

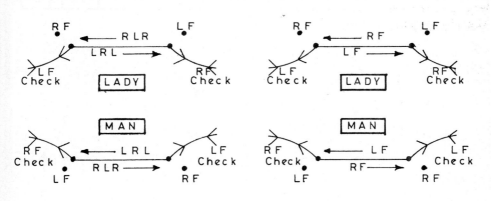

Cha Cha Cha   **Rumba**

There are other forms of the New York. In the Jacqueline Cha Cha Cha both partners are in shadow position with right and left hands joined. They move across the line of dance performing the same steps – "on the same leg". Another variation is the <u>Change of Place</u> – after checking, the partners cross in front and behind moving across the line of dance (Commador Cha Cha Cha (1992)).

The Hand-to-Hand

The hand-to-hand is a backward movement in fallaway position followed by a chasse or side step.

Hand-to-Hand (Man's Steps)		Beat value	
Cha Cha Cha	Rumba	CCC	Rumba
1. RF bk in open fallaway] ¼ turn to R	1. As Cha Cha Cha] ¼ turn to R	1	1
2. Replace wt to LF] ¼ turn to L 3-5. Chasse RLR]	2. As Cha Cha Cha] ¼ turn to L 3. RF to side]	1 ½½1	1 2
etc.	etc.		

(Lady's steps opposite)

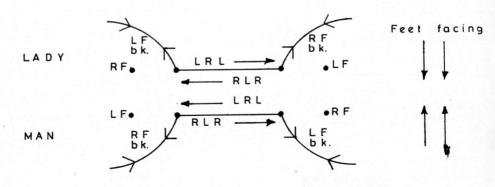

Cha Cha Cha

54

CHAPTER 10

CHASSÉ TURNS

The Quarter Turns

The four quarter turns are standard figures in the
quickstep. They are usually taken along the line of
dance.

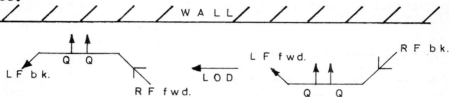

1. Quarter Turn to Right   **3. Progressive Chasse(to left)**

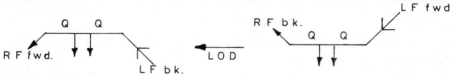

2. Tipple Chasse   **4. Progressive Chasse to Right**

		Man's Steps				Turn
		1	2	3	4	
1	Quarter Turn to Right	RF fwd	LF to side	RF closes to LF	LF to side sltly bk	⅛ R over 1, 2 R over 2, 3
2	Tipple Chasse	LF bk	RF to side	LF closes to RF	RF to side sltly fwd	¼ R over 1, 2
3	Progressive Chasse	RF bk	LF to side	RF closes to LF	LF to side sltly fwd	¼ L over 1, 2
4	Progressive Chasse to R	LF fwd	RF to side	LF closes to RF	RF to side sltly bk	⅛ L over 1, 2 ⅛ L over 2, 3
	Timing	S	Q	Q	S	

Lady's steps for (1) are (2); for (3) are (4) and vice versa.

55

Notice that in (1) and (4) the man is moving <u>forward</u> on the <u>outside</u> of the turn; the turn takes place over all three steps. In (2) and (3) he is moving <u>backward</u> on the <u>inside</u> of the turn and turns on the first two steps.

The Florentine Quickstep (1992) starts with a single change step followed by a quarter turn to the right. The Eivona Quickstep starts with a progressive chasse to the right and has double tipple chasses and double progressive chasses. Progressive chasses are common in waltzes.

Quarter Turn to the Left

The term "quarter turn" is sometimes used for a quarter turn to the right followed by a quarter turn to the left. If this figure is to be followed by a natural figure or a movement outside the partner, the turn to the left is achieved by a progressive chasse. Thus the turn is:-

<u>Quarter Turn to Right and Progressive Chasse</u>

This is the usual quarter turn used in the blues.

In the quickstep it is more common to use a special <u>quarter turn to the left</u> in which the man uses a <u>heel pivot.</u> This is a type of compact chasse in which the turn occurs on the heel of the right foot without transfer of weight.

	Quarter Turn to Left				Timing
	Man's Steps		**Lady's Steps**		
Heel pivot	1. RF bk	¼ turn to L	1. LF fwd	⅛turn to L	S
	2. LF starts to close to RF		2. RF to side		Q
	3. LF closes to RF ww		3. LF closes to RF	⅛turn to L	Q
	4. RF fwd		4. RF bk		S

The Florentine Quickstep (1992) finishes with this figure.

The Naming of Quarter Turns

Quarter Turn	Body Turn	Man's Sideways Chasse Motion
1. Quarter Turn to Right	Right	To Left
2. Tipple Chasse	Right	To Right
3. Progressive Chasse	Left	To Left
4. Progressive Chasse to Right	Left	To Right

Notice that:-

Quarter Turn to the Right is named by body turn.

Progressive Chasse to the Right is named by direction of foot movement in the chasse - it is really a quarter turn to the left.

Tipple Chasse is described in some scripts as Chasse R or even Progressive Chasse R. "Tipple Chasse" is sometimes used to indicate a side chasse with a sway - Waltz Clinique (1991), Blue Dawn Waltz (1991).

These names have arisen from history but are confusing for the beginner.

Turning Chasses

The turning chasses consist of the first three steps of the four quarter turns with a turning movement of 1/4, 3/8 or 1/2.

1. (Slow)	2. (Quick)	3. (Quick)
Pivoting to L or R (Forward or backward)	Step to side still turning	Feet closing together

The Suzanne Quickstep has two forward and two backward chasses with a quarter turn on each to give a reverse chasse square.

The Emmerdale Waltz has a similar reverse square with all steps slow. Other old sequence dances such as the Waltz Marie and Catherine Waltz use four bars for a complete turn but do not divide the turn into four equal parts. Most sequence dancers seem to turn in time to the music and use the last turn to adjust their alignment.

Chasse Reverse and Natural Turns

Chasse turns are standard figures in the quickstep; they are turning chasses with 3/8 turn.

Turns	Man's Steps			Amount of Turn
	1	2	3	
1. 1 to 3 Chasse Reverse	LF fwd	RF to side	LF closes to RF	$\frac{1}{4}$ R over 1, 2 $\frac{1}{8}$ R over 2, 3
2. 1 to 3 (Chasse) Natural	RF fwd	LF to side	RF closes to LF	$\frac{1}{4}$ L over 2, 3 $\frac{1}{8}$ L over 2, 3
Timing	S	Q	Q	

Lady's steps are opposite with the 3/8 turn over the first two steps (inside of turn).

(1 to 3 of the natural and reverse turns in the waltz have exactly the same steps but a SSS timing – see Chapter 11.)

A forward and a backward 3/8 turn together will give an overall turn of 3/4 which is popular in both the waltz and the quickstep. For a reverse turn this will start diagonal to centre (DC) and finish diagonal to wall (DW). (Alignments opposite for the natural turn.) These turns (without a chasse) are standard figures in the waltz.

The forward and backward chasse reverse turn is a common figure in the blues. The Chandella Quickstep starts with this turn. In ballroom dancing the backward chasse turn is usually replaced by a figure involving a heel pivot as in the quickstep quarter turn.

The following figure is the standard reverse chasse turn in the quickstep.

Reverse Chasse Turn				Timing
	Man's Steps		**Lady's Steps**	
	1-3. Chasse Reverse Turn		1-3. Chasse Reverse Turn	SQQ
	4. RF bk		4. LF fwd ⎤ ¼ turn	S
Heel	5. LF starts to close ⎤ ⅜		5. RF to side ⎤⎦ to L	Q
	to RF	turn	6. LF closes to ⎦ ⅛turn	
Pivot	6. LF closes to RF ww ⎦ to L		to RF ⎤ to L	Q
	7. LF fwd		7. RF bk	S

A convenient compromise often used in modern sequence dancing is to follow 1 to 3 of the chasse reverse turn by a progressive chasse to achieve 5/8 of a turn. The Cameron Quickstep (1984), Quatro Quickstep (1991), Katrina Quickstep (1992) and Linden Swing (1992) all start in this way. So does the Denverdale Waltz (1992) without the first chasse - it is easy to remember the start of these dances!

The <u>natural (chasse) turn</u> in the quickstep has a <u>heel pull</u> instead of a heel pivot in the backward figure with a SSS timing.

Natural Turn (Quickstep)				Timing
	Man's Steps		**Lady's Steps**	
	1-3. Chasse Natural Turn		1-3. Chasse Natural Turn	SQQ
	4. LF bk ⎤ ⅜		4. RF fwd ⎤ ¼ turn	S
Heel	5. RF almost closes	turn	5. LF to side ⎦ to R	S
	to LF ⎦ to R		⎦ ⅛ turn	
Pull	6. LF fwd		6. RF bk ⎦ to R	S

The Universal Quickstep and Kontiki Quickstep (1986) have 1-3 of the natural turn followed by a tipple chasse to give a turn of 5/8 (just the opposite of the chasse reverse turn and progressive chasse described above).

Rotary Chasses

The rotary chasse (two-step) is an old-time figure which usually involves a forward turning chasse followed by a backward turning chasse. A half turn is made on each figure giving a complete turn. The Yearning Saunter (1919), Sindy Swing (1984) and Columbine Saunter (1991) all have right rotary chasse turns.

Although very simple in principle, the amount of turn is too large for a really elegant figure. Most dancers seem to swivel on their feet to obtain the correct degree of turn as the feet are closed together. Many dancers use rotary chasse turns instead of the more traditional waltz turns in the final bars of old-time sequence dances such as the Veleta and Military Two-Step.

CHAPTER 11

DANCING TURNS

Closed Turns

Closed turns have the feet together at some stage. This occurs on steps 3 and 6 in the reverse and natural waltz turns.

Reverse Turn		Timing	
Man's Steps	**Lady's Steps**	**Waltz**	**Chasse**
1. LF fwd ⅓ turn to L	1. RF bk ³/₈ turn	S	S
2. RF to side ⅛ turn	2. LF to side to L	S	Q
3. LF closes to RF to L	3. RF closes to LF	S	Q
4. RF bk ³/₈ turn	4. LF fwd ¼ turn	S	S
5. LF to side to L	5. RF to side to L	S	Q
6. RF closes to RF	6. LF closes to RF ⅛ turn	S	Q
	to L		(Ch.10)

(Steps are opposite for the natural turn)

The Denverdale Waltz (1992) starts with a 1 to 3 reverse turn; Hadrian's Waltz (1992) ends with a 4 to 6 reverse turn. Although the foot movements seem simple in these turns they are not easy to execute with proper style. A ballroom teacher would point out many features not immediately apparent to the beginner.

In the Basic Reverse Tango Turn the man's feet are crossed on the third step although the lady closes. This turn with an open finish is found in the Telecon and Trafalgar Tangos (1992).

Open Turns

In open turns the feet pass one another instead of
closing.

Open Reverse Turn		Timing
Man's Steps	**Lady's Steps**	**Foxtrot**
1. LF fwd ⎤ ¼ turn	1. RF bk ⎤ ⅜ turn	S
2. RF to side ⎦ to L	2. LF closes to RF⎦ to L	Q
3. LF bk ⎤ ⅛ turn	3. RF fwd	Q
4. RF bk ⎦ to L	4. LF fwd ⎤ ¼ turn	S
5. LF to side, ⎤ ⅜turn	5. RF to side ⎦ to L	Q
sltly fwd ⎦ to L	⅛turn	
6. RF fwd in CBMP OP	6. LF bk in CBMP ⎤ to L	Q

In this foxtrot open reverse turn the man walks round
without closing whilst the lady does a heel turn on
step 2.

The Saunter Shakara (1992) has 1-3 open reverse turn and
4-6 open reverse turn later. The Cameron Quickstep and
Washington Waltz (1991) have open natural turns.

Steps 4 to 6 are called a "feather finish".

The open reverse turn with open finish in the tango is a
similar turn with a different timing. The Torque Tango
(1991) has this figure.

The Weave is a type of open reverse turn often taken from
promenade position. It is used in the Waltz Clinique
(1991) and Grosvenor Foxtrot (1991). (The natural weave
has the same ending as the weave but turns first right
and then left. It is a type of zig-zag figure used in
foxtrots, e.g. Harlequin Foxtrot (1990)).

The Natural Spin Turn

Natural Spin Turn		Timing	
Man's Steps	Lady's Steps	W	Q

1–3. Natural Turn
4. LF bk, ⎤ ½ turn
  RF in CBMP ⎦ to R
5. RF fwd ⎤ ⅜ turn
6. LF to side, ⎦ to R
  sltly bk
	1–3. Natural Turn
	4. RF fwd ⎤ ½ turn
	  (pivoting action) ⎦ to R
	5. LF bk, sltly to L ⎤ ⅜ turn
	6. RF diag fwd having ⎦ to R
	  brushed to LF
		SSS
		S
		
		S
		S
			SQQ
			S
			
			S
			S

W = Waltz/Q = Quickstep

Step 4 is the <u>pivot</u> which is a turn on the ball of one foot in which the other foot is kept in front after a forward step in CBMP.

Steps 5 and 6 are the <u>spin</u>.

The spin turn is very popular in both the waltz and the quickstep. The Katrina Quickstep (1992) has steps 4 to 6 following a curved feather.

Natural and Reverse Pivot Turns

The <u>natural pivot turn</u> is steps 1 to 4 of the natural spin turn (Margie Quickstep (1990)). The Washington Waltz (1991) has the natural pivot step; the Florentine Quickstep (1992) has a reverse pivot.

The Impetus Turn

Impetus Turn		Timing		
Man's Steps	**Lady's Steps**	**F**	**W**	**Q**
1-3. Natural Turn	1-3. Natural Turn	SQQ	SSS	SQQ
4. LF bk, ⎤ ³⁄₈turn	4. RF fwd ⎤ ³⁄₈turn	S	S	S
5. RF closes to LF⎥⎤ to R	5. LF to side ⎦⎤ to R	Q	S	S
6. LF to side, ⎥ ¼ turn	6. RF diag fwd having ¼ turn	Q	S	S
sltly bk ⎦ to R	brushed to LF ⎦ to R			

F=Foxtrot/W=Waltz/Q=Quickstep. Man's steps 4 and 5 are a heel turn.

The impetus turn can be seen as an alternative to the spin turn. The <u>open impetus turn</u> has step 6 replaced by a diagonal forward step into promenade position; the lady moves to the side in promenade position after a brush step. The White Heather Foxtrot (1991) has 4 to 6 of the impetus turn with a feather ending; the Blue Lace Waltz (1991) has the same figure with an open finish. The Waltz Clinique (1991) has a full open impetus turn, the Queslett Quickstep (1992) has steps 4 to 6 followed by a lock step.

The Reverse Corte

In some respects the first three steps of the reverse corte may be seen as the opposite to the impetus turn with a turn to the left instead of the right.

1 to 3 Reverse Corte		Timing
Man's Steps	**Lady's Steps**	
1. RF bk ⎤ ³⁄₈turn	1. LF fwd ⎤ ¼ turn	S
2. LF closes to RF ww⎦ to L	2. RF to side ⎦⎤ to L	S
3. Position held	3. LF closes to RF ⎥ ⅛turn	S
	to L	

The Bluebird Waltz and Apple Blossom Waltz (1992) have 1 to 3 of the reverse turn followed by the 1 to 3 of the reverse corte.

The Quick Open Reverse Turn

This is a basic reverse turn danced to a quicker rhythm with the lady outside on the third step.

Quick Open Reverse		Timing
Man's Steps	**Lady's Steps**	**Quickstep**
1. LF fwd] ¼ turn 2. RF to side] to L ⅛ turn 3. LF bk in CBMP] to L	1. RF bk] ⅜ turn 2. LF to side,] to L sltly fwd] 3. RF fwd in CBMP OP	S Q Q

(Quatro Quickstep (1991), Sheridan Waltz (1990)).

Telemark Turns

The name "telemark" is taken from a swing turn in skiing. Telemark turns are large, compact turns used with great effect in the slow foxtrot. They are also standard figures in the waltz.

Closed Telemark		Timing	
Man's Steps	**Lady's Steps**	**W**	**F**
1. LF fwd] ⅜ turn 2. RF to side] to L 3. LF to side,] ⅜ turn sltly fwd] to L	1. RF bk] ⅜ turn 2. LF closes to RF] to L 3. RF to side,] ⅜ turn sltly bk] to L	S S S	S Q Q

W = Waltz/F = Foxtrot. The lady's second step is a heel turn.

The April Foxtrot (1992) has a telemark turn followed by a feather step. The Waltz Wynette (1985) has a telemark followed by a 1 to 3 natural turn. The Appleby and Chandella Quicksteps (1990) have closed telemarks.

The open telemark is a telemark turn finished in promenade position; the man turns more than the lady.

Open Telemark			Timing	
Man's Steps		Lady's Steps	W	F

1. LF fwd ⌉ ¼ turn
2. RF to side ⌡⌉ to L
3. LF to side ⌡ ½ turn
   in PP   to L
		1. RF bk ⌉ ⅜ turn
		2. LF closes to RF ⌡ to L
		3. RF diag fwd
		   in PP
			S
			S
			S
				S
				Q
				Q

W = Waltz/F = Foxtrot.

The Woodside and Emmerdale Waltzes and the Apple Blossom Waltz (1992) all have open telemark turns followed by a hover from promenade position and a contra check. The White Heather Foxtrot (1991) and the Tempro Foxtrot (1992) both have an open telemark followed by 1 to 3 of the open natural turn. There is an open telemark in the Tango Torviscas (1992).

The Nevada Foxtrot (1990) starts with a Hover Telemark — the dancer "hovers" on the second step instead of turning.

The Wetheral Waltz (1990) and Harlequin Foxtrot (1990) have Natural Telemarks.

The Top Spin

Top Spin			Timing
Man's Steps		**Lady's Steps**	
1. LF bk in CBMP ⎤ ¼ turn 2. RF bk ⎦ to L 3. LF to side, ⎤ ¼ turn sltly fwd ⎦ to L 4. RF fwd in CBMP OP		1. RF fwd in CBMP OP ⎤ ¼ turn 2. LF fwd ⎦ to L 3. RF to side ⎤ ¼ turn ⎥ to L 4. LF bk in CBMP ⎦	Q Q Q Q

The Nevada Foxtrot (1990) and the White Heather Foxtrot
(1991) both end with a check forward with the right foot
followed by a top spin. The Waltz Rabanne (1992) has a
top spin following a closed impetus turn.

The Outside Spin

Outside Spin			Timing
Man's Steps		**Lady's Steps**	
1. LF bk very small step in CBMP (Pivot) ⎤ Whole 2. RF fwd in CBMP OP ⎥ turn 3. LF to side, ⎥ to R and with LF bk ⎦		1. RF fwd in CBMP OP ⎤ Whole ⎥ turn 2. LF closes to RF ⎥ to R 3. RF fwd between ⎦ partner's feet	S S S

Outside spins are found in Callam's Waltz (1990),
Hadrian's Waltz (1992) and in the Fortuna Foxtrot (1990).

INDEX OF DANCING FIGURES